Approval Voting in the Balance

Guy Ottewell

ISBN 978-0-934546-78-2

The cartoons are by Ian Dicks (ian@dicks-chamberlain.co.uk).

The cover picture is a sunset painting I made of the agora at Athens,
birthplace of democracy.

Universal Workshop

www.universalworkshop.com

Durham, North Carolina, U.S.A., and Isleworth, Middlesex, England

Contents

4	Preface
5	The arithmetic of voting
13	The other AV (2011)
18	Examples of the need
20	An ample example (2019)
22	Where approvl voting has been used
24	Approval, disapproval, and neither
25	Voting for boards
26	Activists for approval voting
27	Exit polls; an X-ray into viting systems
28	An exit poll in New Mexico (2018)

Preface

The gist of the idea
Approval voting is the system in which you are allowed to vote for more than one.

It proves to be more fair than the common system, called plurality voting, in which each voter can vote for only one candidate or option even if there are more than two.

History of the idea
The earlier title of this pamphlet was "The Arithmetic of Voting." I drafted it in 1964, in Manchester, including the diagrams as shown here; wrote it fully in February 1968, in Los Angeles passing it to friends for comment. Eventually I printed it in my magazine *In Defense of Variety* (4, July-August 1977).

The only discussions of voting systems I had seen were in the June 1976 *Scientific American* and subsequent correspondence. The solutions that were mentioned did not include approval voting, and, in strong contrast with its simplicity, were elaborate – requiring re-counts, or second rounds, or after-the-vote analysis by computers. This was the provocation that made me get my article into print.

Unknown to me, the idea was put forward by several others about the same time: John Kellett and Kenneth Mott ("Presidential Primaries: Measuring Popular Choice," in *Polity*, Summer 1977); Robert J. Weber ("Comparison of Voting Systems," mimeographed, 1977); Steven J. Brams and Peter C. Fishburn ("Approval Voting," *American Political Science Review*, September 1978); and Richard A. Morin (*Structural Reform: Ballots*, New York, Vantage Press, 1980).

The expression "approval voting" was coined by Weber. I had touched on this aspect ("Giving one vote each to every candidate you don't mind electing ...," "The votes ... really represent the numbers of people who are *not against* them") but I had forgotten to think of a handy term.

To that original "Arithmetic of Voting" essay I have added other pieces, and a more focused title.

The Arithmetic of Voting

"One man shall have one vote."   So said John Cartwright, in *People's Barrier Against Undue Influence*, 1780.

But one of the consequences of this seemingly sacred rule is that the more good options there are (candidates, parties, or measures) the weaker each becomes, and the weaker they become collectively.

Let us suppose that there are two political sides, A and B. If there is one candidate on each side, and if the one-person-one-vote rule applies, perfect justice prevails. That is to say, the division of the vote corresponds exactly to the wishes of the people. If, for instance, the people are exactly divided between A and B (as is unlikely but possible), then the result is a draw, which is awkward but just. For justice in an election means that the division of the votes comes out proportional to the divisions among the voters.

But what if another candidate enters on side B? Philosophically we might think that this ought to strengthen that side. But of course it does just the opposite. If, as before, 50 percent of the people are for A and 50 percent for B, then the two B candidates will now divide 50 percent of the vote between them. They will get perhaps 25 percent each; at any rate, each will get less than 50 percent; and so A will win, not because there are more voters on that side, but because there are more candidates on the other side. If a third candidate enters on side B, the average vote received by the candidates will be divided by three, and so on.

Another way of putting it is that if there are two candidates altogether A needs over half the votes to win; if there are 3, he or she needs over 1/3; if 4, only 1/4; and so on.

Let us tabulate the situation in a simplified form, imagining that there are four voters, and two "sides," and the voters are evenly divided between the sides. With one candidate on each side, the result is:

voters:	1	2	3	4	total
A	1	1			2
B			1	1	2

With one side split:

	1	2	3	4	total
A	1	1			2
B_1			1		1
B_2				1	1

Or the split may be of this kind:

	1	2	3	4	total
A	1	1			2
B_M			1		1
B_E				1	1

– where the notations "M" and "E" mean "moderate" and "extreme."

Originally I drafted these ideas in February of 1968. At that time A could be imagined to be Nixon, B_M Johnson, and B_E King, or McCarthy, or the Peace and Freedom Party; or, conversely, A could be Johnson, B_M Nixon, and B_E Wallace. That situation has long since passed, but it might be less invidious to think in some such terms than to suggest contemporary equivalents.

I do not apologize for infusing the idea of "good" and "bad" sides into such a discussion. Of course there is never a side that is the good one in everybody's view, and so it is utterly non-objective to identify one side as the good one. In any specific election, however, and in the minds of individual voters, the sides are good and bad in varying degrees. The very institution of elections assumes this, for it asks the voters to identify the opton they consider the good one. From a general point of view, the purpose of elections is the lofty and impartial one of ensuring that the majority wishes of the people are respected; but from most individual points of view the far more vitally felt aim is to ensure that the Republicans (or Socialists, or Christian Democrats ...) get into power. And neither purpose is truly served by the rule of one-person-one-vote.

The whole thing can be stated in a dispassionate way, without reference to "good" or to "sides": if, out of three or more candidates, two are similar, and even if a majority of voters prefers either one of these, yet the votes of that majority are split between them, with the result that another candidate is likely to win, though not wanted by the majority.

The primary reason why this seems wrong is that it makes the result of the vote depend more on the distribution of the candidates than on the distribution of the voters' wishes. Secondly, it is the opposite of the way it should be in that candidates ought to be encouraged, not discouraged, from adding their names to the competition; each new candidate may be an improvement on the others; at any rate the voters have a wider choice, and the statistical chance of electing a good candidate is higher.

Thirdly, you have only to think of the dilemma you are placed in if you happen to be one of the voters supporting side B, especially BE, and especially if it is a relatively small splinter. If there had been only two candidates, you would have voted for the one you considered better. To them is added another whom you consider better still, but he has less chance to win. If you do vote for him, you have in effect given your vote to the candidate you consider worst. On the other hand you feel that if you and others like you do not vote for the one you believe in, his cause will never have a chance to grow.

All this is well known. It is "a fact of political life"; it is "the voter's dilemma." Heads are shaken over it at almost every election. It is used: there are many instances in which one side has encouraged extra candidates to run on the other side, even "planted" them there, in order to divide that side. Or, conversely, a side "undivides": Labour and the Liberal Democrats make a pact not to run against each other in certain constituencies, so that they each will have more chance of beating the Conservatives; this is called "tactical voting." Because it is known and exploited, do we have to accept it?

First solution that doesn't work
Let each voter cast as many votes as there are candidates.

The result then might be like this:

A	3	3			6
B_1			2	1	3
B_2			1	2	3

That is, it would be essentially the same as before. Voters on the side where there is only one candidate would give all their votes to him; those on the side where there is more than one candidate either would divide their votes, or would divide among themselves, some giving all their votes to one candidate on the side and some to another. This is in effect the one-vote system still, except that your one vote may be divided into fractions of a vote.

Second solution that doesn't work

Let each voter put the candidates, or as many as he wishes to vote for, in order — 1st, 2nd, 3rd. Count his first choice as 3 votes, his 2nd as 2, his 3rd as 1.

Result:

A	3	3			6
B_1			3	2	5
B_2			2	3	5

Again, the average of the votes for each candidate on the divided side is inevitably lower than the number of votes for the one candidate on the undivided side.

One of the candidates on the divided side could come out level with the candidate on the undivided side, but only if *every* voter on his side puts him first:

A	3	3			6
B_1			3	3	6
B_2			2	2	4

Third solution that doesn't work

Let each voter cast as many votes as he likes, up to some predetermined number, such as 10.

This is really just a variant of the first solution, with the number of votes per voter changed. And so the result will be essentially the same:

A	10	10			20
B_1			6	3	9
B_2			4	7	11

These first three solutions are really all weighted-vote systems. In the first and third, the voter determines the various kinds of weight he can give to his own votes; in the second, it is determined in advance for him.

Solution that works

Let each voter cast as many single votes as he likes, provided they are all for different candidates.

Result:

A	1	1			2
B_1			1	1	2
B_2			1	1	2

This is stalemate, as it should be in the hypothetical situation where the two "sides" are exactly equal. If, as would happen in reality, one of the two sides has slightly more adherents than the other, then one of the candidates on that side will win. The "splitting" of side B between two (or more) candidates has not lowered the potential number of votes for each of those candidates.

This system can be seen as negative voting. Giving one vote each to every candidate you don't mind electing is equivalent to voting, instead, against everyone you do not want to see in office. Thus in our example the two voters who voted for both B candidates could be said to have voted against A.

With three candidates, you could cast up to three votes; but casting all three would have the same effect as not voting at all. As this shows, a voter casting more than one vote does not exercise more power. Indeed, if there is just one candidate you want to help, you can do so most powerfully by casting only one vote.

Thus far I have been simplifying to the extreme. What kind of difference will it make when, instead of imagining that there are two clear-cut "sides," we deal with the possibility that there is overlap between them? Or when the numbers of their supporters, instead of being small and equal, are large and irregular?

Here is a somewhat more flexible kind of tabulation, which will allow us to play with examples of these more real and complicated situations:

candid-ates	percentage of supporters	present system, various possible results				
A	40 / 10	40%	50%	50%	40%	45%
B_M	30 / 15	55%	30%	45%	40%	43%
B_E	5	5%	20%	5%	20%	12%
total:		100%	100%	100%	100%	100%
candidate accepted by majority wins		yes	no	no	?	no
real strength of candidates shown		B_M	A	B_E	A,B_E	none

In this particular situation, 40% of the electorate supports only A, 30% only the moderate B, and 5% only the extreme B. 10% are the "floating" or potential "cross-over" voters, the ones who don't mind voting for either Democrat or Republican (say) but want to keep the extremists out.

15% are the ones who would perhaps prefer the extreme B, but may realistically have to support the moderate B if they want to keep A out.

The result under the present system can vary widely, because of what these latter two groups may choose to do. The 15% group may opt for either BM or BE, depending on how they decide to resolve the rather agonizing dilemma we referred to already. This is really a tactical decision; it is not an ideological one. And really therefore it is not the sort of thing that voters should be asked to decide: they are supposed to be voting in order to express their preference; they should not be asked to make calculations of expediency which should be part of the job of the politicians themselves or of political analysts. The 10% group may opt for either A or BM; they are not in a dilemma, or at least not of the same tactical kind – they opt one way or the other because of the latest speeches of the candidates, or trends of the economy, and these are indeed matters that should concern the voter.

In practice, of course, the 10% group will split, in any one of an infinity of different proportions; so may the 15% group; so there are not five possible results but an infinity. This kind of unpredictability in results is not a sign of some kind of richness in the present system, but is a sign of failure in it. We must distinguish between two kinds of variation: variation in the underlying numbers of people who feel in sundry ways; and variations in what may result, given one pattern of those numbers. Here we are imagining that, like God, we know the underlying pattern: 40% feel in favor of A only, and so on. Given this pattern, there should ideally be one result, expressing the wishes of the people; not a variety of possible results, expressing merely the fact that some people are forced into a dilemma.

Under the proposed system, such people can vote for both the candidate they really want and the next-best candidate who has a better chance of winning. There is (given our still rather simple "underlying pattern of wishes") one possible result. And from a count of the actual votes cast for A only, for A+BM, and so on, it would actually be possible to reconstruct our table that sets out the "underlying pattern of wishes." No longer will only God know it!

The numbers of votes the three candidates get really represent the numbers of people who are not against them. That is why they add up to more than 100%: many voters are not-against more than one candidate.

In the particular example, BM is the candidate with the largest number of people for, or rather not against, him; so under the proposed system he wins. Under the present system he could win but is more likely (given the structure of our numbers) to lose to A.

BE is the "extreme" candidate with the smallest support. In the present system he may end up with only his hard-core supporters voting for him (5%). This is not really fair: he has more sympathizers than that; but with so little actual help from their sympathy his cause may wither away. His votes can range up to 20%, the actual amount of his sympathizers, but only as an unlikely upper limit. In the proposed system, however, he receives 20% of votes. He still comes third, but the amount of support he has is actually expressed in votes, and he can proceed to build from there.

Another type of political situation can be represented like this:

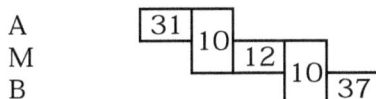

```
A        ┌──┐
         │31│┌──┐
         └──┤10│┌──┐
M           └──┤12│┌──┐
               └──┤10│┌──┐
B                 └──┤37│
                     └──┘
```

Here M (a notation that evolves easily out of our BM) is a small party of the middle. (The parties might be thought of as the British Labour, Liberal, and Conservative.) In the traditional system M can receive up to 32% of the vote, but is likely to receive little more than 12%, since its sympathizers in the two 10% groups fear that they will be throwing away their votes unless they give them to the large parties. A can receive from 31% to 41% and B from 37% to 47%, so it is uncertain which of them will win, the uncertainty depending on which way the 10% groups resolve their dilemmas. The traditional system is therefore unfair to the middle in a situation like this. In the proposed system, A gets 41%, M 32%, B 47%; B wins, as it should, and M gets a proportion of votes that shows the extent of its support fairly.

You are welcome to think of other situations and analyze them by means of the same sort of diagram; perhaps more insights will emerge about the weaknesses or strengths of the suggested system.

There are two quite serious criticisms that you may already have noticed; but if you have noticed both of them you may also notice that they are approximately opposite to each other.

The first is that the system favors parties of the middle. The probability that a middle-of-the-road party will win is increased over that probability in the present system, because, in the proposed system, people from the areas both to right and to left of it can more readily vote for it: while still preferring, and still voting for, a party on the flank, they can also vote for the party in the middle without fearing that they are damaging their own flank party.

The other criticism is that the proposed system favors parties of the extremes! Actually this applies to any small, relatively unsuccessful, or new party. Instead of giving it only the small number of votes representing its hard-core support — the people who insist on voting for it even while knowing that it has no chance of winning — the system will tend to give it the larger number of votes representing the people who don't mind it, or prefer it, because they can vote for it without detracting from their support of the larger next-best party.

Probably no decision about an electoral system is without its effect on the outcome — no change in voter-registration procedures, district boundaries, ballot apparatus, or any other matter of method, is pure of effects on the actual fortunes of Republicans, Tories, or whoever is concerned. A change in method whose possible effects are to put into office parties that the fewest people object to, and to show the true extent of the support for all parties including the small ones, seems as benevolent as any.

This form of voting is the second simplest after one-person-one-vote. It is time to give this costless reform a conspicuous trial.

This piece was drafted before the referendum it discusses, was offered in shorter forms as a letter to newspapers, and was revised after the failure of the referendum.

The Other AV

The British referendum of May 2011 on electoral reform was a long-awaited chance for the country to grow out of its ancient voting system. That system has always seemed simple and obvious; yet, whenever there are more than two candidates, it produces unfair results.

But the only method people were allowed to choose instead was not the best. It was rejected, probably not on its merits but because it was complicated enough to cause confusions and suspicions.

There was another system that was scarcely talked about, though far simpler and in several respects better.

Terminology (dammit!)

First – though I hate to have to do so – I must say something about the names of these three voting systems.

The ancient system is known as Majority Voting or Plurality Voting, but is often called, and was so designated in the referendum, First Past the Post. This, besides being clumsy enough to stumble over (how many times have people said or written FTPT instead of FPTP?), is a metaphor and an inaccurate one. It doesn't mean that whoever first reaches a certain number or "post" wins; it means that whoever gets the most votes wins. It used to be known just as One Man One Vote, so I call it One Person One Vote, OPOV.

The best and next simplest system is called Approval Voting. That describes it well enough. It means that the winner is the one that the largest number of voters are willing to accept.

The system offered in the referendum was being called Alternative Voting. There are three objections to that term. It did nothing to describe the system. It (deliberately?) suggested that the system was the only alternative – which was far from true. And tt the AV acronym from Approval Voting, whose name dates back to 1977.

So I have to put it in quotation marks: "AV." Henceforth, AV without those marks will mean Approval Voting only.

"AV" was actually one of the many forms of Preferential Voting. It is used in three countries, Fiji, Papua New Guinea, and Australia, though the form of it used in Australia is even more complicated. In the USA and elsewhere it is called Instant Runoff Voting – which does not mean that it produces an instant result, only that the "runoffs" are not separate elections (as they are in France). It has also been called Ware's Method, and by other names.

What is wrong with One Person One Vote?

It forces you to choose between a candidate who could win and a candidate you might really prefer. From the point of view of the individual, this is "the voter's dilemma" or the problem of whether to "vote tactically"; from the point of view of a party or philosophy, it is the problem of the "split vote" and of "spoilers."

And it often allows candidates to win though they are approved by only a minority, indeed by fewer than other candidates are.

Solving these two problems – the split vote and the unrepresentative win – is the core purpose of electoral reform.

Consider the common situation in which A or B could win and C has only an outside chance; you are horrified by A, you could live with B, you would most like C.

If you give C your "heartfelt" vote, you make it more likely for B to lose to A. If you give B your "realistic" vote, the true extent of support for C won't be known, and C may fade out. And even if B and C together get more votes than A, A is likely to wins.

What is Preferential Voting ("AV")?

You may vote for as many of the candidates as you wish. You must number them in order of preference. If no candidate gets at least 50% of first preferences, then the candidate with the smallest number of those is eliminated and that candidate's ballots are redistributed to the remaining candidates according to the next preference on each ballot. This process is repeated until one of the remaining candidates gets at least 50% of the remaining votes.

The result is an improvement in that you can give a form of your "heartfelt" vote in addition to your "realistic" vote, and the winner will usually (not, as proponents claim, always) have been voted for by more than 50%, whether as first or other preferences.

Confusions, misperceptions, suspicions

Sure, it isn't as complicated as astrophysics. But it's complicated enough to go wrong.

Most people need to read the explanation at least twice, and many itncluding me, don't grasp it well enough to remember it accurately. Easy enough to understand that you must write "1," "2," "3," etc. But it is not easy to feel sure of what will happen to your vote afterwards, as it travels that process of redistributions. If voters do not clearly imagine the consequences of what they do, the democratic nature of the system is somewhat in doubt.

I've talked with well-educated people who did not realize that you don't have to rank all the candidates. Even the Yes to Fairer Votes campaign, which promoted the referendum, could get it wrong: I went to a meeting at which we were invited to fill in sample "AV Ballot Papers" so as to see how they worked, and the instructions on them were: "Put a number next to each candidate ... until all candidates have been given a nuwtmber"!

The instructions went on: "The higher the number, the less you favour them, much like a top 5 list of favourites." For there is a danger of voters getting that wrong – giving the highest number to the favored candidate – and thus doing the exact opposite of what they intend.

And there is the non-negligible risk of voters spoiling their ballots, by inadvertently writing two 2s, or a 3 and a 5 but no 4.

The Electoral Commission's booklet, distributed a month before the referendum, looked like a desperate effort to deconfuse the public. It took four pages to explain the "Alternative Vote," with pictures of piles of ballot papers.

So would the redistributings be done in a flash inside computers, or by manual re-counting as those pictures suggested, and how long would it take? Getting answers to those questions was not easy; in fact it took me weeks of unanswered and partly-answered questions sent to officials. The only answers were that the Electoral Commission did "not plan to introduce any voting machines"; and that the Bill decreeing the referendum required that, after each round of redistributing and re-counting (in each constituency), the detailed numbers should be made public. This suggested a cumbersome process nationwide.

A conspicuous example of a mistaken idea came from no less a statesman than David Owen, leader of the former Social Democratic Party, in an article in *The Independent on Sunday* (13 March 2011): " ... the second preferences of the least popular candidates have the most influence. Because the first candidate to get eliminated under AV – typically a fringe or extremist candidate – gets their votes redistributed first, they have the best chance of determining the final result." Wow, that sounds like a penetrating criticism that we hadn't thought of! But think it through. It doesn't matter that the 14th strongest party's votes are the first to get redistributed, since the 13th, of which there are more, will get redistributed next, and so on up to the 3rd. If Lord Owen could get lost in the logic, anyone could.

Two deeper questions about Preferential Voting ("AV")

What if you write only a "1," as you are entitled to, because there is only one candidate you wish to vote for – and that candidate gets eliminated? To whom will your vote be reassigned? Answer: To nobody. It is thrown away, or as the Electoral Commission said "is not used."

More broadly, this is what happens if neither of the candidates who survive to the last round is one to whom you've given a number. Your vote can only be reassigned to someone to whom you've given a number. So it will not be part of the final totals. Otherwise, it would be possible for A, B, and C all to end with totals of less than 50%. So we should more truly say that the winner will have been voted for by at least 50% of those whose votes count. The rest of the voters were disenfranchised.

And: What effect will it have if you rank the candidates you approve – B and C, say – as 1 and 2, or the other way around? Will you still disadvantage the one to whom you don't give your first preference? It took me quite a bit of figuring with various scenarios before I realized that it makes no difference. Whether you rank C as 1 or 2, your vote will eventually go to B. More generally, for all of the names that you approve, it doesn't matter which number you put beside any of them! It's a decision you are forced to make, sometimes a dilemma, but a dilemma whose resolution doesn't matter.

So why rank at all? Why not just tick?

Approval Voting

That is what is done in Approval Voting, which has been described by me and other authors since 1977, but has been used, without being called by a specific name, in various elections since ancient times. It is essentially the system used in almost all elections for members of boards and other councils.

In Approval Voting, as in "AV," you can vote for as many candidates as you wish. The difference is that you don't have to rank them. If there are four, you can vote for one or two or three. Of course voting for all would have the same non-effect as voting for none. As in One Person One Vote, whoever gets the most votes wins. That's all.

Suppose that roughly 40% approve Conservative only, 30% Labour only, 15% Liberal Democrat only, and 15% approve both Labour and Lib Dem, in either order. Then the approval totals are Conservative 40, Labour 45, Lib Dem 30.

Given the distribution of the voters' real wishes, there is – unlike under One Person One Vote, "AV," or any other system – only one possible outcome. That "distribution of the voters' real wishes" is made manifest in those simple figures.

"AV" records it with finer detail – but detail that varies according to how voters resolve their unnecessary dilemmas, and detail that is impractical to publish. It might take up a whole page to report that in a certain constituency "X voted for Green 1, Conservative 2, Lib Dem 3, BNP 4 ... , Official Monster Raving Loony Party 15" and all other actual combinations.

Various other situations – kinds of distribution of the voters' wishes – are explored in *The Arithmetic of Voting*.

Surprising simplicity

Approval Voting has been described as "a surprisingly simple costless reform." It is the next simplest after One Person One Vote, in that nobody has to do any ranking; it is simple and costless in that the ballots are counted once, there is no redistributing, no re-counting.

It sounds surprising, in that you can vote for more than one and the votes add up to more than 100%. But, just as in the elections for boards, where you may vote for six people out of twenty, nobody who votes for two or more candidates has more power over the result than those who vote for only one.

A pleasant advantage of Approval Voting over "AV" is that people can have real-life experiences of it at any time, thus becoming comfortable with it. A situation arises in which a group of people has to select three out of nine options — say, as the short-list for further action, or recipients of an award. Or even just one option out of three. (Which book shall we read for the next book club meeting? Which park shall we go to for our picnic?) They each write down as many of the options as they think fit. They soon have the result.

"Alternative Voting" would be no alternative, because utterly impracticable.

The future

What about Proportional Representation? Many regard it as the real reform beyond "AV." But it is not a method of casting votes; it has to do with the number of seats being voted for. If a region is to have 10 seats, then those can be shared among parties in proportion to the numbers of votes cast under One Person One Vote, or (much more fairly) under Approval Voting. But not under the intricate results of "AV," because only the first preferences could be used (think, for instance, of the false result for voters who rank not some but all of the options). So the voter's dilemma would be reintroduced; in fact, the system would reduce merely to a needlessly complex version of OPOV.

If from "AV" we had gone on to get Proportional Representation, we would have to go back to using OPOV as the voting method. Unless ... I say no more.

AV was rejected by the 2011 referendum. Those who have not given up on real reform would be well advised to begin listening to the few small voices that have been trying to call attention to Approval Voting. This "surprisingly simple costless reform" has been consistently shut out of discussion, presumably because its surprisingness has prevented commentators from noticing its elegant soundness.

Examples of the need

Here are a few examples of situations that cried out for Approval Voting: elections in which a "side," at least as perceived by many people, was split.

The 1992 British general election offered a classic Voter's Dilemma. In opinion polls, Conservative and Labour were neck-and-neck at about 40 percent; the Liberal Democrats had 16%. Actually, 35% wanted Lib Dem, but 19% of those feared to "waste" their vote: if they voted for Lib Dem, Conservative would win; if they voted for Labour, Lib Dem would never get the benefit of their support. (Conservative won.)

In the 1992 U.S. presidential election, the popular votes for Bill Clinton (Democrat), George H.W. Bush (Republican), and Ross Perot (independent) were 44,909,889; 39,104,545; and 19,743,821. .Bush and Perot were both conservative (and both at times led in the early polling). Clinton's final margin over Bush was much smaller than the number who voted for Perot. If all or many of those who supported Bush and Perot had been allowed to vote for both, Bush would have won.

In the 2000 U.S. presidential election, George W. Bush (Republican) and Al Gore (Democrat) respectively got 50,456,002 and 50,999.897 votes, but 30 and 20 states in the Electoral College, so that Bush was the winner though losing the popular vote. But Ralph Nader (Green) won enough votes that he was considered by many, though not all, to be a "spoiler." If in swing states such as Florida a few hundred who voted for Nader had instead voted for Gore, or been allowed to vote for Gore also, the presidency would have gone to Gore.

(Because of this prospect, some supporters of the Gore-Nader "side" made exchanges: a person in Florida agreed to vote for Gore, who could possibly win there, if a correspondent in South Carolina would vote for Nader, who had no chance of winning there.)

In November 2002, there was a special election to fill, for only four weeks, the seat of Hawaii's recently deceased Representative in Congress, Patsy Mink. There were 38 candidates — 12 Republican, 11 Democrat, 11 non-partisan, 2 Green, 2 Libertarian. As remarked by John Flanigan, who sent me this example, "It's likely that the winner will get far fewer than half, and in the exceptional case, might win with as little as 3% of the vote! Was there ever a better candidate for Approval Voting?" In other words, the strongest Republican (say) could have lost votes to all the other Republicans who might have been well liked by individual voters. However, one of the Democrats won with 51%.

In Egypt's 2005 presidential election, Hosni Mubarak, who had been in power for four six-year terms, and Ayman Nour were thought to have support of about 35% each. There was a third candidate, Nu'man Gumaa, who was said to have about 20%, but was seen as a government-backed spoiler, set up to weaken Nour. In the result, whose fairness was contested, Mubarak got an improbable 88.6%, Nour 7.3%, and Gumaa

2.8%. If the pre-election estimates were realistic, then under approval voting Nour should have won with 55%.

In the Copeland constituency of Cumbria in northwest England, in the general election of 2015, the Labour candidate was expected to win narrowly — unless the right-wing UKIP withdrew in order not to pull votes from the Conservative. UKIP did not withdraw; Labour won by 2,564, which was less than the 6,148 who had voted for UKIP.

In the Democratic Republic of Congo, in November 2018, seven opposition parties agreed to co-operate by backing just one "joint" candidate, the "widely respected" Martin Fayulu. In that way they would be able to end the rule, since 2001, of Joseph Kabila. Probably Fayulu was approved by more than half of the electorate. But within a day the agreement collapsed: some of the parties decided they couldn't agree to have their own candidates excluded from the ballot. Under approval voting, they would have been able to vote both for their own candidates and for Fayulu.

In the U.S. in January 2019, Howard Schultz, billionaire former chief executive of Starbucks, declared his candidacy for president as "centrist independent"; he said that "Nobody wants to see Donald Trump removed from office more than me," but Democrats perceived that he could split the vote against Trump.

In a by-election at Peterborough in England in May 2019 (at almost the same time as the European Parliament elections), four pro-Europe parties — Liberal Democrat, Green, Renew, and Change UK — tried to avoid the split vote by uniting behind one candidate. Feverish talks failed to reach agreement by the four o'clock deadline for registering.

In the August 2019 by-election for the Welsh constituency of Brecon and Radnorshire, the Liberal Democrat candidate was able to defeat the Conservative — because other parties, Green and Plaid Cymru, which agreed with the Liberal Democrats on the major issue of the time (remaining in the European Union), helped by not fielding candidates. There were complaints that this was a "dirty trick." With approval voting, the fair result would have been achieved without it.

In each of these situations, large proportions of the population suffered the "voter's dilemma." I have suffered it in at least the last eight of the major elections in which I have been a voter.

There are many more examples, and they will continue to pile up.

An ample example

Seats in the European Parliament are filled by the system of proportional representation. Each constituency is a fairly large region, and is represented by a number of members (MEPs). Each political party can submit a list of one or more candidates. The parties win numbers of seats depending on the number of votes their slate receives.

Thus the South West England constituency consisted of the city of Bristol, the counties of Gloucestershire, Wiltshire, Somerset, Dorset, Devon, and Cornwall — and Gibraltar! It had 6 seats in the parliament.

On the ballot for the May 2019 election were 11 parties. They could be divided into: Liberal Democrat, Green, and Change UK, all "remainers," opposed to Britain's withdrawal from the European Union; United Kingdom Independence Party, Brexit Party, and English Democrats, all "leavers," objecting even to membership in the parliament; Conservative and Labour, the nation's major parties, both divided on the issue; and three Independents, philosophy unknown (to me). All parties were fielding 6 candidates in a numbered order, except the English Democrats with 2, and the one-person Independents.

And the instruction: "Vote for only one." An acute dilemma! If I'm pro-Europe, do I vote Green and take a vote away from Lib Dem? Or, if I'm "euroskeptic," do I support the new Brexit Party, thus weakening Ukip? Both "sides" are triply split. This will have been replicated in many other constituencies.

The Liberal Democrats had pleaded with the Greens and the newly formed Change UK to make common cause. It didn't happen, and all that could be done was to circulate tips on how to vote tactically in various regions.

This case illustrates not only that both "sides" — virtually all of the population — can be badly in need of approval voting, but also that AV is perfectly compatible with the other greatly needed electoral reform: proportional representation, which enables minority philosophies to have somebody speaking up for them. You will see definitions of approval voting, such as in Wikipedia, that start by saying it is used in "single-winner" elections. Not only. It is perfectly suitable when there are to be multiple winners, as for boards of directors and for the European parliament.

The result, in the South West region, was that the Brexit party got 36.84% of the vote and 3 seats, the Lib Dems 23.19% and 2 seats, the Greens 18.21% and 1 seat. The others got no seats — not because they got below 10% but because there were only 6 seats.

However, the votes for the three unequivocally Leave parties (Brexit, UKIP, English Democrats) added to 37,35%, and for the three unequivocally Remain parties (Lib Dem. Green. Chamge UK) 44.31%.

Election of Members of the European Parliament for the South West Region

Vote **only once** by putting a cross **X** in the box next to your choice

!

Change UK - The Independent Group

1. Rachel Sabiha Johnson
2. Jim Godfrey
3. Oliver Sean Grevatt Middleton
4. Matthew Hooberman
5. Elizabeth-Anne Sewell
6. Crispin Hunt

X

Conservative and Unionist Party

1. Ashley Peter Fox
2. James Michael Mustoe
3. Faye Purbrick
4. Claire Michelle Hiscott
5. James Taghdissian
6. Emmeline Elizabeth Owens

Conservatives

English Democrats

English Democrats - Putting England First!

1. Jenny Knight
2. Michael Thomas Martin Blundell

English Democrats

Green Party

1. Molly Scott Cato
2. Cleo Alberta Lake
3. Carla Suzanne Denyer
4. Tom Scott
5. Martin John Dimery
6. Karen Margaret La Borde

Green Party

X

Labour Party

1. Clare Miranda Moody
2. Andrew Adonis
3. Jayne Susannah Kirkham
4. Neil William Guild
5. Yvonne Margaret Atkinson
6. Sadik Adam Al-Hassan

Labour

Liberal Democrats

1. Caroline Jane Voaden
2. Martin Charles Horwood
3. Stephen Roy Williams
4. Eleanor Anne Christine Rylance
5. David Nigel Chalmers
6. Luke Oliver Stagnetto

Liberal Democrats

X

The Brexit Party

1. Ann Noreen Widdecombe
2. James Alexander Glancy
3. Christina Sheila Jordan
4. Ann Christine Tarr
5. Roger Charles Lane-Nott
6. Nicola Jane Darke

BREXIT PARTY

UK Independence Party (UKIP)

UKIP Make Brexit Happen

1. Lawrence James Webb
2. Carl Benjamin
3. Anthony James McIntyre
4. Lester Geoffrey Taylor
5. Stephen Alaric Lee
6. Alison Jane Sheridan

UKIP

Maxey, Larch Ian Albert Frank

Independent

Rahman, Mothiur

Independent

Seed, Neville

Independent

We should be allowed to vote like this.

Where approval voting has been used

Informal processes that are essentially approval voting are often used when groups of people decide on something, such as which restaurant to go to.

There have been political uses of AV, or close equivalents, before the system was described or the term was invented.

In Venice, from 1268 to the end of the Venetian republic in 1797, the Doge was elected through a ten-stage process of which several stages were random; the complexity prevented conspiratorial ways of gaining the powerful position. The final stage, reached by 41 electors, was a form of AV: each of the 41 proposed one candidate; these were discussed and examined; then each elector cast votes for as many of the candidates as he approved; the winner was he who received most votes, provided that these were at least 25.

Popes were elected by AV from 1294 until 1621. 41 popes and some of the anti-popes were elected this way. A simplified description is that the first round of secret voting in the conclave might produce a winner with a majority of more than two thirds; otherwise, there were successive rounds in which the electors lowered their standards, voting for increased numbers of candidates, until someone reached the two-thirds bar. The process was intended to prevent some of the notorious scheming, corruption, and violence. It did on the whole produce better popes – though the pope who introduced it, Celestine V, resigned after five months and was imprisoned and murdered by his successor!

The first four U.S. presidential elections (1788, 1792, 1796, 1800) used a kind of reduced AV. Each elector could vote for up to 2 of the up to 13 candidates. The 1800 result was that the winner and runner-up, Thomas Jefferson and John Adams, became president and vice president; as they hated each other, the system was then changed, though it had been the runner-up-becomes-vice-president custom that caused the problem, not the voting method.

In Greece in 1864, the method of electing members of parliament was changed from plurality voting to approval voting, partly because it had previously been used in the prosperous Ionian Islands, which became part of Greece in that year. AV continued till 1926, when it was replaced by proportional representation, probably because the ruling party had not liked the result.

In China, the huge National People's Congress has since 1979 been elected by a process that is approval voting with some modifications: mainly, that to win a seat a candidate must get more than 50% approvals; if none does, the seat is left vacant.

Approval voting has been used by U.S. political parties for their internal elections. Pennsylvania's Democratic State Committee conducted a presidential straw poll by AV in 1983. The Boston Tea Party, which sprang up in 2006, specified in its by-laws that "The method of voting shall be 'Approval Voting.' Each voting member may cast one vote for every candidate which he or she deems an acceptable nominee to the office" of president or vice president; with a further process if no one received more than 50%.

In the late 1980s, communist countries of eastern Europe used approval voting in thousands of elections. The Soviet Union under Mikhail Gorbachev, as an experiment toward democratization, held AV elections — the largest ever, so far — on 21 June 1987 in about 2,500 of its 50,000 villages, towns, and districts. Voters "disapproved" candidates rather than "approving" others — mathematically identical though psychologically perhaps different. The experiment did not continue, because Gorbachev and the Soviet Union fell in 1991.

Elections to Cuba's National Assembly, such as that in 2003, may use an AV system, since sources about them seem to show that large numbers of candidates received more than 50% approval.

Bills to adopt AV have been introduced in several U.S. states. The book *Approval Voting* by Steven J. Brams and Peter C. Fishburn, 1983, includes a "Bill to Enact Approval Voting in New York State." In North Dakota a 1987 bill passed the state Senate but not the House. Oregon in 1990 used AV in a referendum on school financing, letting voters approve as many as they wished out of five options. In 2007 Colorado state representative John Kefalas introduce a bill that would have allowed municipalities to use AV in non-partisan elections; the bill passed the state committee but died in the appropriations committee because of lack of funding for legal research.

Fargo, North Dakota's largest city, held a referendum on 6 November 2018, by which this became the first city in the U.S. to adopt approval voting. The vote was 30,041 to 17,264 (64% to 36%) — more of a "landslide" than any U.S. president has ever achieved.

Gallup polls and other opinion surveys frequently use questionnaires of the approval voting kind, asking respondents to choose as many as they like out of a list of candidates. Such polls have shown that the actual results of many American elections have been distorted, in that less-approved or even least-approved candidates have won.

Warren D. Smith gives detail on this in parts of his large website (https://rangevoting.org/USA2016retro.html and https://rangevoting.org/RangePolls.html). He advocates Range Voting or Score Voting, which is like AV with the addition that numerical scores are given to candidates. But one part of his website is called "A Paean to approval voting," and I am indebted to him for giving me pointers to many of the instances of the use of AV in history.

Approval, disapproval, and neither

In approval voting, you give a Yes to as many as you like. (Or a No to the others.) There is a variation in which you can give a Don't Know, or No Opinion, to those on which you have no opinion. It seems only one step less simple. Actually, it entails casting three kinds of vote instead of one.

Anna Louise Strong, an intrepid American tourist of political systems, wrote an account of North Korean elections she observed. The national election of 1949 was a one-party confirmation, but she also described a village committee election that used three-way approval voting. There were 12 candidates for 5 positions; each voter received 12 cards on each of which was the name of one of the candidates. "He then cast his chosen ones into the white box and the rejected ones into the black." Into either box he could throw any number of cards from one to twelve. And: he could walk home with some of the cards, having not voted those candidates either up or down. The Korean War broke out in 1950; such voting may or may not have survived the turmoil.

The Secretary general of the United Nations is chosen by approval voting with the third option. In 2006, for example, the 15 member nations of the Security Council cast "encourage," "discourage," or "no opinion" votes for 6 candidates. Ban Ki-Moon won by receiving 14 approvals, 0 disapprovals, and 1 no-opinion. Another difference from AV is that any one of the five permanent members (U.S., Britain, France, Russia, China) can veto the result.

The middle-ground option is attractive. In many elections, especially those with a large number of candidates, there are liable to be some about whom you know nothing. Giving them a No can be unfair; it pushes their future chances downward, whereas gving them a No Opinion leaves them on a level. Voting in this triple way might be almost as easy to explain. Howevr, counting the votes would be more complex. The three kinds of marks on ballots would have to be counted as 1, 0, and -1.

Voting for boards

The method typically used in elections to bodies such as boards of directors is a kind of approval voting manqué. Voters are told to vote for up to, say, 6 out of a list of 12.

The number is arbitrary and unnecessary, even if it corresponds to the number of posts to be filled. The instruction could be "one or more" or "as many as you like." It would be better: you might want to vote for 7 or 8 because you know them to be good; you then have the problem — a version of the usual voter's dilemma — of deciding which one or two to reject. Voting for more than 6 would not result in more than 6 people being elected.

Voting for all 12 candidates would have as little effect as turning in a ballot with no checkmarks — except that doing either, rather than not voting at all, could be said to contribute to the amount of voter participation. In elections to the board of Amnesty International U.S.A., a complaint is that only 4 percent of members vote. That may be because most members don't know any of the candidates; a member who does know them all and knows that they are all good people might want to vote so.

Many scientific and technical societies have adopted full apprival voting for their board elections. Some large ones are the Institute of Electrical and Electronics Engineers (with over 400,000 members), the Mathematical Association of America, the American Mathematical Society, the Institute for Operations Research and Management Sciences (INFORMS), and the American Statistical Association.

Activists for Approval Voting

The Center for Election Science (CES) is a non-profit founded in 2011 in the U.S.A. It backs, and campaigns for, AV. It creates educational materials, sponsors peer-reviewed research, and has worked with other non-government organizations to help them adopt AV for their internal elections. Among the useful features of its website, electionscience.org (formerly electology.org), are an electoral system glossary, a classified "library" of articles about voting systems, and a sort of magic-balloons page where you can click on one of the "problems" ("hyper-partisanship," "suppressed ideas," "tactical voting," "vote splitting," "spoiler effect," "bad candidates") and see its "solution" appear.

In February 2013, CES created a video about AV and entered it in a contest for a grant from the McArthur Foundation, which was looking for ideas on how to "strengthen American democracy." In 2018, CES worked with the group Reform Fargo that succeeded in getting AV introduced in that North Dakota city. In March 2019, the Open Philanthropy Project awarded CES a $1,800,000 grant to continue advocacy of AV. And in May, CES made a grant to St. Louis Approves, for educational work toward introducing AV in St. Louis, Missouri (population over 300,000).

In February and March of 2001, John Flanigan, professor of mathematics at Kapiolani Community College in Hawaii, mailed a copy of *The Arithmetic of Voting* with a cover letter (and with much toil and expense, shared by Jim Metz and by students) to every member of the U.S. Senate and House of Representatives. John's Washington-experienced brother predicted that without sizable donations there would be little result, and indeed responses came only from the offices of the Hawaii senators and one congressperson. John has also sent letters explaining AV to papers such as the *Los Angeles Times*.

Exit polls: an X-ray into voting systems

Exit polls, in which voters are questioned as they leave voting stations, are usually carried out to give early indications of which way elections are going, but they can also shed light on the tendecies among the voters, why they made their choices, and what they would have done in different circumstances.

In the French presidential election of 2002, 16 candidates all received less than 50% (the highest was 19.9%), so by the French rule there had to be a runoff between the top two, Jacques Chirac and Marine Le Pen. Chirac won this by an enormous margin. But, in exit polls, several thousand voters were asked how they would have voted if they could have used approval voting. Results showed that Le Pen would have come a poor 4th; 2nd would have been Lionel Jospin, a popular former prime minister, who might well have won in the runoff. It was suggested that some Chirac supporters voted for Le Pen, to increase the likelihood that she would be the easily-defeated opponent in the runoff. If so, that was a glaring example of tactical voting. Many of the other candidates, who helped to split the actual vote, would have fared differently.

Similar exit poll studies were carried out by academics, with government funding, at the French presidential elections of 2007, 2012, and 2017, showing what the results would have been under AV and other systems.

What was in effect an exit poll was conducted on 21 January 2008 at Messel, a small town near Frankfurt in Germany. It was part of a study by researchers from the University of Konstanz, supported by the German government. Alongside the ordinary voting at three polling stations, 1,009 people voted in the Approval way. The ordinary voting was dominated by the nation's two leading parties, the CDU and SPD/ In the Approval voting, "third parties" did strikingly better. It was clear that people favoring for instance the Greens had decided against voting for them for fear of "wasting" a vote and helping the wrong established party. The authors of the study wrote:

"With the Approval Voting System, the notion of the 'two big parties' seems less appropriate to describe the political situation. There were in fact 4 parties which received an approval rate above 30%: the CDU, the SPD, the Greens and the FDP. On this basis, the results of a state election would have produced four major factions, each with a similar number of seats in Parliament. One could even infer on this basis that the official vote's splitting of voter preferences into two political sides is an artificial product of the voting system."

An exit poll in New Mexico

Jan Kok and Blake Huber conducted an exit poll at two voting centers in Albuquerque, New Mexico, during the U.S. mid-term election on 6 November 2018. Jan is a co-founder of the Center for Election Science and was its first vice president. Blake was the 2016 vice presidential candidate for the Approval Voting Party.

The candidates for a senate seat in New Mexico were the incumbent, Martin Heinrich, Democrat; Mick Rich, Republican; and Gary Johnson, Libertarian. Since the Democrats and Republicans are nationally the major parties, Johnson had to be regarded as a "third party" candidate. But he was a strong one, because well known, having been governor of the state, as a Republican, and candidate for the U.S. presidency in 2016, as a Libertarian. So this was a good test case of the difference that voting systems might make when there are more options than two.

Jan and Blake worked from 9 a.m. till the polls closed at 7 p.m. They asked people coming out of the polling stations to mark survey forms, similar to ballots, but with these instructions in English and Spanish: "Please indicate how you voted just now" and "Please indicate how you would vote if you could vote for as many candidates as you like."

Among the 313 people who completed the forms, 51.4%, 28.4%, and 19.2% had voted for the Democrat, the Republican, and the Libertarian respectively. (The results of the whole election were similar but even more skewed toward the major parties: 54.1%, 30.5%, 15.4%.)

But, if these people had been allowed to vote for more than one, the proportions would have become 54.3%, 28.4%, and 40.6%. The difference is seen clearly in Jan's bar chart: blue and orange represent the percentages of actual votes and Approval votes among this sample of voters.

It is evident that a large number of voters approved both the Democrat and the Libertarian, but were forced to vote for either one or the other. Only 19.2% did vote for the Libertarian. A further 21.4% — a greater number — would have done so if they could, but did not, quite likely fearing that their votes would be "wasted" or would hand victory to the candidate they least approved.

The incumbent Democrat won anyway, as was probably predictable. The Libertarian came last. Under Approval Voting, he would have come second, and the amount of his real support would have been made public.

It is a considerable surprise to find that a "third" party is, more truly, second, with a level of support as high as 40.6%. It's a surprise of a kind that may be hidden within many election results. If true levels of support were manifest, parties and candidates would be able to grow in a manner based on their merits.

Exit poll results, Plurality vs. Approval Voting

2018 New Mexico US Senate race

Note the much higher results for the alternative party candidate with Approval Voting!

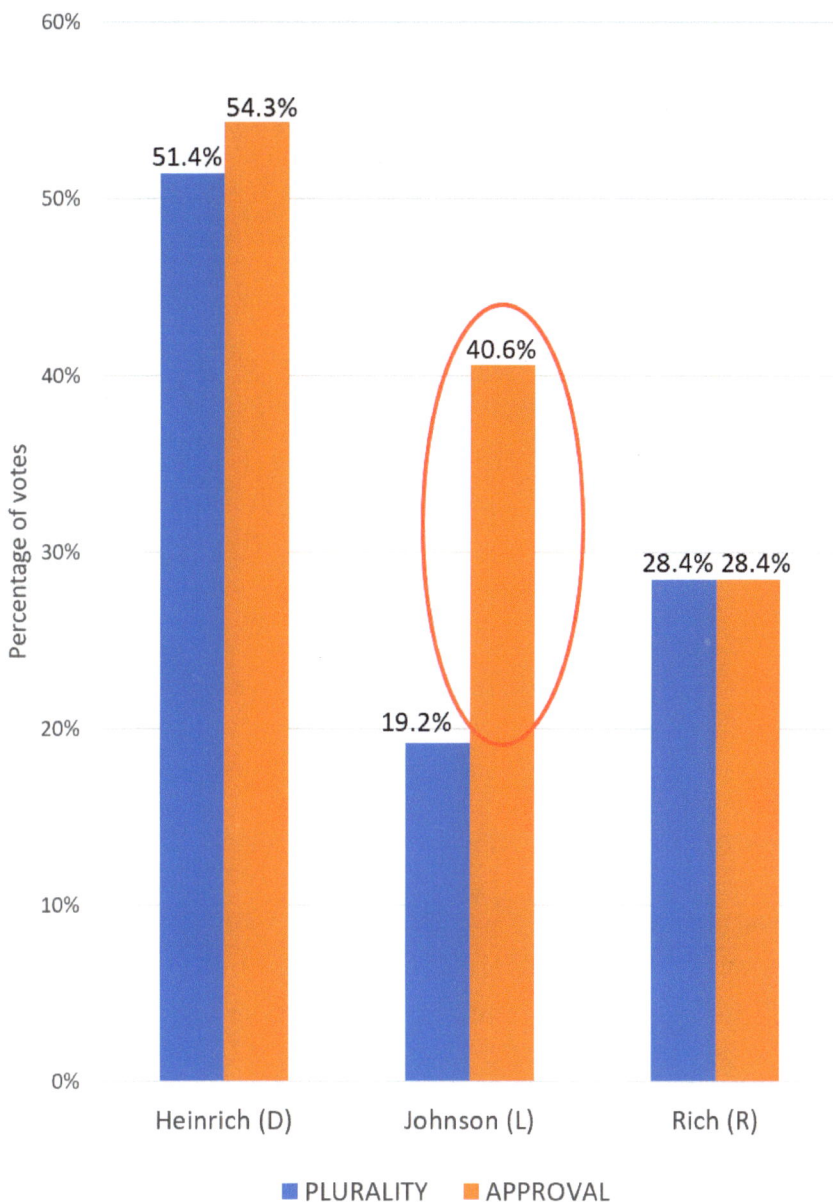

When I asked my friend Ian Dicks for a cartoon, his first version didn't quite get the idea. Approval Voting doesn't mean that you just cast a lot of votes!

www.ingramcontent.com/pod-product-compliance
Lightning Source LLC
Chambersburg PA
CBHW041223270326
41933CB00001B/31